Head...
Gl...

With Your Mates

Written by Hiawyn Oram
Illustrated by John Aggs

Turn to page 23 to read

Forgiving Florence

Published by Pearson Education Limited, Edinburgh Gate, Harlow, Essex, CM20 2JE
Registered company number: 872828

www.pearsonschools.co.uk

Text © Hiawyn Oram 2011

Designed by Bigtop
Original illustrations © Pearson Education 2011
Illustrated by John Aggs

The right of Hiawyn Oram to be identified as author of this work has been asserted by her in accordance with the Copyright, Designs and Patents Act 1988.

First published 2011

15 14 13 12
10 9 8 7 6 5 4 3

British Library Cataloguing in Publication Data
A catalogue record for this book is available from the British Library

ISBN 978 1 408 27400 2

Copyright notice
All rights reserved. No part of this publication may be reproduced in any form or by any means (including photocopying or storing it in any medium by electronic means and whether or not transiently or incidentally to some other use of this publication) without the written permission of the copyright owner, except in accordance with the provisions of the Copyright, Designs and Patents Act 1988 or under the terms of a licence issued by the Copyright Licensing Agency, Saffron House, 6–10 Kirby Street, London EC1N 8TS (www.cla.co.uk). Applications for the copyright owner's written permission should be addressed to the publisher.

Printed and bound in Malaysia, CTP–PJB

Acknowledgements
We would like to thank the children and teachers of Bangor Central Integrated Primary School, NI; Bishop Henderson C of E Primary School, Somerset; Brookside Community Primary School, Somerset; Cheddington Combined School, Buckinghamshire; Cofton Primary School, Birmingham; Dair House Independent School, Buckinghamshire; Deal Parochial School, Kent; Newbold Riverside Primary School, Rugby and Windmill Primary School, Oxford for their invaluable help in the development and trialling of the Bug Club resources.

Every effort has been made to contact copyright holders of material reproduced in this book. Any omissions will be rectified in subsequent printings if notice is given to the publishers.

Ben Balshaw is brilliant at football. He can play in any position. He can head a ball half-way down the pitch. His shooting can be so cool it's as if he were out in the street casually kicking a can into a hedge.

Our team coach tries not to praise him too often and make the rest of us feel bad, but you can see it in his eyes. From Coach's eyes shine the words 'brilliant' and 'natural talent' and 'thank goodness for Ben'.

Florence Arrowsmith is the other one. She is just about as fast as a cheetah – the fastest land animal on Earth. One minute this end of the field, the next minute the other, having dribbled the ball all the way as if it were glued to her boot. **(Unlike me, Ethan Brown. Whatever I've got on my feet – boots, astros or trainers – footballs seem to run the other way.)**

But anyway, here's the bad news. Apart from Ben and Florence, there was no one else in Hollyfield Primary's team – our team – who could play for toffee. Zip. Zero. Nobody.

Coach didn't say that though, of course. He didn't need to. The fact was, and we all knew it, there were only four weeks until the District Competition, and even *with* Ben and Florence on the team we were … sorry to say it … rubbish. Not just a 'Quarter Pound of Rubbish' as they'd nicknamed Queens Park Rangers (which isn't true – they're ace). No, we were more like a whole pound of rubbish. A triple whopper of no-win uselessness.

And still we hoped. Of course we did. So did Coach. We hoped for a miracle. We hoped we'd try harder, train harder, do more stretches, do more sit-ups, set up goals better, pass better – especially pass to Ben better.

And, anyway, with Ben and Florence in the team, we had a chance, didn't we? A small chance maybe, but still a chance. **_Didn't we?_**

We did, but then, in the time it takes to cough twice, that small chance was halved.

Florence's mother flounced in to see the Head and the next thing it was official. Florence Speed-of-Cheetah Glue-Boot Arrowsmith was leaving.

Coach looked sick as a sick dog when he told us. She was leaving – completely leaving – to go to the Arndale Academy, the school with the best football team in the whole county – in fact, the reigning champions!

She was going there because her mother thought her talents were too good to waste. Too good to waste *in a team as useless as ours* was part of what she meant, even if no one was rude enough to say it.

Except for Florence.

She said it straight to our faces the day she left, laughing and flicking her cheetah-coloured hair. She didn't care. Why should she? She had a magic boot and the pace of the fastest land animal on Earth.

Only then, it got worse. Far worse.

Ben's dad was something big in Broad Elm Rangers Football Club and he organised this CHARITY MATCH DAY. There were lots of different matches and one was Broad Elm Rangers Under 11s against Brushey Park FC Under 11s. Ben had to play for the Broad Elm team, of course, and as I'm always round at his house and they needed one more player, I got roped in.

And this is when disaster struck.

Two Broad Elm talent scouts were there! They stood with Ben's dad on the touch line and watched as Ben scored – not one, not two, but **three** brilliant goals. Two of them headers. (How does he do it, you have to ask?)

After the match they called Ben over and stood in a huddle and talked.

Ben's dad had his arm around Ben's shoulders. He couldn't have been prouder. You could see it a mile off.

With mud on my face and mud in my heart I went to change. I had a horrible feeling that if Ben went to play for the Club he wouldn't be able to go on playing for Hollyfield – *our team*. And one thing was certain – if he wasn't playing with us, and with Florence gone too, we'd be knocked out of the

District Competition in the very first match.

Wipe-out.

And no matter how many times Coach said *'it isn't the winning, it's the taking part that counts'*, we were normal. We wanted both. We wanted to take part AND win.

I changed slowly so I'd still be there when Ben came in. Although I didn't want him to join Broad Elm Rangers, I was his friend. I had to be there to congratulate him if he had been chosen.

I hung around pretending I couldn't find one shoe – but Ben didn't come to change. Instead, his dad came and collected his clothes.

"Hey, Ethan!" he said. "Great match. And you kept up. Well done. These Ben's things? Can we give you a lift home?"

I had my bike there so I said no thanks. Then I peered out of the changing room and saw them drive off in their car. I don't know what came over me but I didn't go straight home. I followed.

They got to their house well before me and when I arrived they were already inside. I slipped through the side gate and went to eavesdrop at the open sitting-room window.

This is what I overheard:

BEN TO HIS DAD: *I don't want to join the Club, Dad. Not if it means I can't play for Hollyfield. Hollyfield's my school. It's my team.*

HIS DAD: *Well, you can't play for both, Ben. The FA sets the rules. Not me. They control how many match-hours kids your age can play.*

BEN: *Then I'm not going.*

HIS DAD: *What do you mean? You've got serious talent and they're a top club. It's the chance of a lifetime, son.*

BEN: *I like playing where I am.*

HIS DAD: *Hollyfield Primary is not a good team, Ben. In fact, it's hopeless. And with Florence gone, you can learn nothing playing with them.*

BEN: *Well the answer is no. I'm not going. (Now shouting) AND YOU CAN'T MAKE ME.*

HIS DAD: *Ben …!*

BEN: *(Now yelling the house down)* *I'M NOT JOINING BROAD ELM RANGERS. I'm staying where I am and I'm playing with my mates. And that's the end of the story.*

I was so shocked by the yelling – Ben is normally as gentle as a well-behaved mouse – **but** so excited, too, that I kicked over a flower pot. It was quite a big pot and the crash was loud.

I was off as fast as my not very fast legs would go, taking with me the most amazing news I could ever expect to eavesdrop on.

Nobody knew the details except me and I wasn't telling.

All everyone knew (because of rumours

which always get out) was this: Ben had been talent-spotted by Broad Elm Rangers but he wasn't going to join them. He was STAYING WITH US. HE WAS PLAYING WITH US.

We were inspired by his total loyalty. Coach was even more inspired.

"Now," he said, "I was up all night thinking and this is what we're going to do. We're going to bring in some players from Year 4. There are three who are very good – Amber Askew, In-su Nang and Mohammed Parmar. I've checked the rules and all three are old enough. However, there is a downside to my idea. It will mean three of you will have to sit on the bench."

I had my hand up lightning fast. "Me, sir. I'll be happy to sit on the bench."

Everyone laughed – but not unkindly. It was no secret that I preferred reading, writing and arithmetic to running.

Big mates Jason Watts and Aarush Rao whispered together. Then up went their hands together.

"And we will, sir. Aarush and me," said Jason.

"That's the team spirit!" said Coach. "Now let's get to work. And yes, that includes the bench-sitters."

The next day, Amber, In-su and Mohammed started playing with us, and they were good. Not brilliant like Ben and Florence, but then no one can be. Obviously.

Two weeks later the matches began. Turn away now if you don't think you can believe the results but this is how they went:

DISTRICT COMPETITION RESULTS

(as in us!)

Hollyfield 2–0 Mayfield
Hollyfield 2–1 Barnsbury Juniors
Hollyfield 3–1 Briar Heath
Hollyfield 2–1 St Vincent's
Hollyfield 3–2 Haydon Hill Primary
Hollyfield 2–0 Shoredown Juniors

All wins for us! Then the deciding match for the District Competition between **OUR TEAM and SOUTH GREEN (AS IN LAST YEAR'S CHAMPIONS)** ... **and** ... wait for it ... final result? The miracle we'd hoped and worked for (or sat and cheered wildly for): **3–2 to us – Ben heading the winning goal straight into the net in extra time!**

"I can hardly believe it," said Ben as we walked back to the bus after the presentation. "We did it. We're the District Champions!"

"Mainly due to you and your ace goals," I said. "And because you stood up to your dad and stuck with us - your mates."

"How did you know about that?" said Ben.

I blushed and told him the truth.

"I was listening from outside. It was me who broke the flower pot!"

He grinned and slapped a muddy arm round my shoulders.

"I had a feeling it was you. And thanks for not spreading it around. You know ... all the yelling and stuff."

"That's OK and thanks for staying," I managed to say through the massive grin that was spreading across my mud-free, bench-sitting, VERY PROUD face.

Heading for Glory

Forgiving Florence

Written by Hiawyn Oram
Illustrated by John Aggs

It's funny how things go. Florence had flounced off to the Arndale Academy with her nose in the air but now it seemed she wanted to COME BACK.

Ben and I and a few others were mucking around in the playground when Louise, Florence's old best friend, came to tell us.

Ben wrinkled his nose but didn't say anything.

I said a lot. I said, "Well, don't think she can just come back in the *team*. She deserted us when we really needed her. Whereas SOME people …" I glanced at Ben … "some people stayed *loyal*, remember?"

Louise said, "For your information, Ethan, it's not just about football, which is all you lot ever think about. She's really *unhappy* at the Arndale."

"So?" said Jason and Aarush together.

"Yes, *so*?" I said. "*We* were unhappy when she said she was too good to waste on a team as useless as ours."

"That was her mum who said that," said Louise. "She was just copying her mum."

"It was," said Sarah, Louise's new best friend since Florence had left. "We heard her."

"Always blame the parents," I said sarcastically.

"No," said Louise, "she REALLY misses her friends here."

No one said it, but Ben and I and the others wanted to say ... **well, we don't miss her**.

Except, and here's the difficult part ... I think deep down we *did* miss her. Her cheetah-coloured hair flying down the field. The ball glued to her magic boot. Her easiness. Her lightness. Her laugh. We were just too hurt by her desertion to admit it.

That was our problem. We were hurt, we weren't going to admit it and we wanted to hurt her back. The usual old thing. Hurt me and see how I can hurt you.

I said, "Well, even if she does come back, there's no guarantee she's back in the *team.* Is there?" I looked round at the others.

"We'll ask Coach what he thinks," said Ben quietly. "This afternoon."

Because we'd had that amazing victory at the District Competition, we were now in the County Competition and had got to the semi-finals.

Coach had us practising EVERY afternoon which wasn't that great for someone like me whose talents definitely do not lie in ball games. Even so, a team is a team, and I went along EVERY afternoon and was never sorry I did.

Anyway, that afternoon, we told Coach the news about Florence.

He stroked his chin and said, "Yes, I've heard about this from the Head. If there's still a place for her here, what do you all think about her re-joining the team?"

None of us knew what to say, now that Coach was expecting *us* to make that decision.

We scuffed at the pitch and muttered things like ... 'don't know' ... 'not fair' ... 'who would we drop?' ... 'team's great as it is'.

"Hmmm," said Coach. "I agree. You're a very **good** team as you are. I couldn't be more proud of each and every one of you. You've worked hard, you've adapted well to Florence suddenly leaving, and you've all been a real credit to yourselves and the team. I don't think I could drop a single one of you in order to give Florence back her position."

We beamed inside. We blushed and beamed at each other. It wasn't often

we got such glowing praise showered down on us like stardust. It made us glow right back – especially as we knew what he said was TRUE.

That afternoon we all warmed up and played as we'd never played before in a practice. I know that because even *I* nearly scored, grazing the post with a low-angled drive. That was a first, I can tell you!

When things are going too well, beware. Put on your protective clothing. Velcro up your knee pads and shin pads. Something unexpected is bound to jump out at you and knock you flat. That's what now happened to our team that was feeling just a bit INVINCIBLE.

Ben went skate-boarding with his older brother and ... BADOOOFF. He was trying to do a Pop Shove-It (no idea what that is but his brother said so) and he came a cropper.

With one week to go before the semi-finals match against the mighty South Green Primary, Ben Balshaw – the best player we are ever likely to have on our side – couldn't play because ... HE'D BROKEN HIS ARM.

He didn't come to school for a week and when he did, weirdly, Florence was back too. Her mother must have somehow sorted it with the Head, because there they both were in assembly – Ben looking embarrassed with his arm in plaster, and Florence looking as light and easy as ever.

Of course, with the semi-final against South Green looming, it didn't take a genius to work out the obvious thing. The obvious thing of Florence coming straight back in the team and playing in Ben's place!

For that to happen, we were going to have to ADMIT how much she'd hurt us by leaving us in the first place. Then we'd have to FORGIVE her – and that wouldn't be easy. Especially because, as far as we could see, she wasn't feeling even one teeny, tiny scrap sorry.

We were all quite sulky when we arrived for practice that afternoon. Florence was there and we stood apart from her.

Coach had us running round to warm up as usual while Ben sat on the sidelines holding his plaster and looking miserable.

Then Coach gathered us round for a team talk.

"OK, boys and girls, decision time. Obviously Ben can't play on Thursday. So this is what we're going to do. Amber will play in Ben's place at centre-back and ..." His eyes came to me, though I was praying they wouldn't ... "Ethan, you'll be off the bench and take over from Amber in centre-mid."

Everyone gasped. One or two giggled.

Then silence fell. He hadn't mentioned Florence. Now he did.

"Florence," he said, "you'll be on the bench."

A huge gasp – the biggest from Florence.

"But sir ... " she said. "I'm ..."

"On the bench," said Coach. "On Thursday and now."

"But, sir ..."

"On the bench," said Coach.

It was pure genius.

I did my best in that practice and played well – for me. My heart was soaring, which helped. It soared all the more when I looked over at the bench and saw Ben at one end and Florence at the other.

After a while, Ben came and stood on the touchline. I liked that even more – seeing Florence alone and looking SORRY. Sorry for herself, OK, but that was surely the start of feeling properly sorry.

And that's all we wanted. For Florence to ADMIT she'd deserted and hurt us and to say SORRY. If she did that, we could start to forgive her.

I was sure this was Coach's plan and had my fingers and toes crossed that it would work.

Was it too much to hope for? Yes.

After practice, Florence flounced off. She changed and was gone before we even got to the changing room. And nothing from her – not one word – of sorry.

The same thing happened on Tuesday and Wednesday, and then it was Thursday, the day of the semi-final, and still Coach hadn't weakened. He hadn't put her back in the team.

None of us could believe it. To win against South Green without Ben, we needed Florence.

We needed her badly. We needed her so badly we were feeling mighty sorry for ourselves about not having her!

In the bus on the way to the big match, we had all completely forgiven her. We waited and waited for Coach to announce she'd be playing.

It didn't happen. He didn't weaken. We were desperate.

"She *has* to play," Ben whispered. "You're the brains round here. Think of something."

"OK," I said. "I'll get a terrible pain."

"Forget it," said Ben. "Coach will know you're faking, right off."

And he did. We were warming up and I fell down and started writhing around.

He came over and helped me up.

"Sudden pain, is it, Ethan? Out of nowhere?"

"Aaaaaahhhhh, in agony, sir," I groaned. "Can't play like this, sir. I'll have to be on the bench. Florence will HAVE to play in my place, sir."

He raised his eyebrows. "Faking's not what we do, Ethan, to get our way in the world, is it?" he said. "*Is it*?"

I stopped groaning. "No, sir, it's not," I said. "It's just that you're being so *hard* on her."

"So you've forgiven her, then, have you?"

"Completely, sir."

"All of you?" said Coach.

"One hundred and ten per cent," I said. "Every single one of us.

"Then leave it with me," he said. "But your playing has improved, Ethan, so you're on first. No way out."

The match started. Less than ten minutes in, I nearly scored one of my just-missed post-grazing goals, and that seemed to satisfy Coach.

Whistles blew and that was that ... I was in my rightful place, back on the bench and FLORENCE WAS RUNNING ON.

You can guess the result. With her cheetah-speed and a magic boot that footballs can't help sticking to, we won that semi-final.

Of course we won, and Florence was back in the team – completely forgiven and her desertion forgotten. Fact is, kids can't hold grudges for long. It's against our nature.

And besides, Florence *did* say sorry in her own sort of light and easy way.

As we waited for the bus back to school she flicked her cheetah-coloured hair and said, "It's so great to be back."

And with a quick smile straight at me, she added. "You guys, all of you … are … the best. And if you ask me, we're heading for glory."